Cold War Choir Practice

a play with music by Ro Reddick

Winner of the Susan Smith Blackburn Prize 2026

methuen | drama

LONDON · NEW YORK · OXFORD · NEW DELHI · SYDNEY

METHUEN DRAMA

Bloomsbury Publishing Plc, 50 Bedford Square, London, WC1B 3DP, UK
Bloomsbury Publishing Inc, 1359 Broadway, New York, NY 10018, USA
Bloomsbury Publishing Ireland, 29 Earlsfort Terrace, Dublin 2,
D02 AY28, Ireland

BLOOMSBURY, METHUEN DRAMA and the Methuen
Drama logo are trademarks of Bloomsbury Publishing Plc.

First published in Great Britain 2026

Cover design: Megan Wilson

A catalogue record for this book is available from the British Library.

A catalog record for this book is available from the Library of Congress.

ISBN: PB: 978-1-3506-3980-5
ePDF: 978-1-3506-3982-9
eBook: 978-1-3506-3981-2

Series: Modern Plays

Typeset by Mark Heslington Ltd, Scarborough, North Yorkshire

For product safety related questions contact
productsafety@bloomsbury.com.

To find out more about our authors and books visit
www.bloomsbury.com and sign up for our newsletters.

Cold War Choir Practice was developed and originally produced by Clubbed Thumb and Page 73 as part of Summerworks 2025 with the following cast and creative team:

Directed by Knud Adams
Music directed by Ellen Winter

Cast: Alana Raquel Bowers, Will Cobbs, Nina Grollman, Andy Lucien, Grace McLean, Lizan Mitchell, Mallory Portnoy, Suzzy Roche and Ellen Winter
Set: Afsoon Pajoufar
Costumes: Brenda Abbandandolo
Lighting: Masha Tsimring
Sound: Kathy Ruvuna
Movement: Baye & Asa
Stage Manager: Christina M. Woolard

Cold War Choir Practice was developed and produced in September 2025 at Trinity Repertory Company, Providence, RI Curt Columbus, Artistic Director, Kate Liberman, Executive Director with the following cast and creative team:

Meek: Lucia Aremu
Puddin': Jackie Davis
Clay: Taavon Gamble
Virgie: Rebecca Gibel
Smooch: Mathieu Myrick
Familiar Face/The Choir: Alison Russo
The Choir/Understudy for Virgie & Familiar Face: Anna Slate
The Choir: Hannah Spacone
Choir Leader/Accompanist: Emily Turtle
Understudy for The Choir: Bethany Aiken, Molly Donovan
Understudy for Meek/Puddin': Autumn Mist Jefferson
Understudy for Smooch/Clay: Tylar Jahumpa

Written by: Ro Reddick
Director: Aileen Wen McGroddy
Music Director: Bethany Aiken

Choreographer: Taavon Gamble
Scenic Design: Michael McGarty
Costume Design: April M. Hickman
Lighting Design: Eric Watkins
Sound Design: Caroline Eng
Puppet Design: Drew Dir, Sarah Fornace
Fight Choreographer: Mark Rose
Stage Manager: Polly Feliciano
Assistant Stage Manager: Olivia Tighe

It was then produced by MCC Theater, Clubbed Thumb and Page 73 in 2026

MCC Artistic Directors: Bernard Telsey & William Cantler / MCC Executive Director: Blake West
Clubbed Thumb Artistic Director: Maria Striar / Clubbed Thumb Producing Director: Michael Bulger
Page 73 Artistic Director: Michael Walkup / Page 73 Interim Executive Director: Renee Blinkwolt

It ran Off-Broadway at MCC Theater, co-produced with Clubbed Thumb & Page 73, February 2026 with the following cast and creative team:

Meek: Alana Raquel Bowers
Smooch: Will Cobbs
Understudy/Choir: Layan Elwazani
Virgie: Crystal Finn
Clay: Andy Lucien
Choir: Grace McLean
Puddin: Lizan Mitchell
Choir: Suzzy Roche
Choir: Nina Ross
Choir Leader: Ellen Winter

Writer: Ro Reddick
Director: Knud Adams
Scenic Designer: Afsoon Pajoufar
Costume Designer: Brenda Abbandandolo
Lighting Designer: Masha Tsimring

Sound Designer: Kathy Ruvuna
Hair Designer: Sarah Jordan
Music Director: Ellen Winter
Orchestrations by: Ro Reddick & Ellen Winter
Movement Direction: Baye & Asa
Props Supervisor: Natalie Carney
DEI Consultant: Nicole Johnson / Harriet Tubman Effect
Production Stage Manager: Christina M. Woolard
Casting by: Clubbed Thumb, Page 73

For Edith and Jeanette

Author Preface

When I was a kid, my best friend's mother would swing by in her station wagon and take Jackie and me to choir practice every week. We were in the local chapter of a Cold War-era children's chorus, and whoever organized this chapter must have had a connection to the local zoo, because that's where we rehearsed, often in a conference room, sometimes in the lobby. We sang about world peace and nuclear annihilation in equal measure. We learned songs in "all the languages of the world", we sang a Song for a Russian Child, we sang to save the world from itself. When rehearsal ended, we climbed back into the car and I returned to a life where my family's concerns were more immediate and the stakes felt just as high.

I was in my second semester of grad school when Putin invaded Ukraine. Think pieces asked if the US had entered a new Cold War. In an art history class we discussed the first Cold War and considered how citizens, then and now, carve out pockets of autonomy when the prerogatives of the nation threaten to overwhelm them. All of this brought my choir memories flooding back. When I shared this story with a playwright friend, she responded, that's a play.

It's rare that you're reminded of a more innocent version of yourself, one that was just starting to understand how much danger the world can hold (and perhaps that's why I sometimes got choked up watching performances). Was I ever really so young? So hopeful? In some ways Cold War Choir Practice is a coming of age story. It's a play interested in the moment when our palms, feeling their way through the dark, hit one of the jagged contours of the world, its sharp edges drawing blood. It's also about how we negotiate our relationship to the groups that sometimes help us, sometimes harm us, but always hold some kind of power over us. More than anything, it's about what we can find just past the sharp edges, if we reach far enough. Another set of hands feeling their way through the dark, ready to clasp our own.

I'd like to thank the brilliant theatermakers who took a chance on producing this play: Maria Striar and Michael Bulger at Clubbed Thumb, Michael Walkup and Kari Olmon at Page 73, and Will Cantler, Bernie Telsey, Scott Galina, and Elissa Huang at MCC. Thank you to Trinity Rep, Curt Columbus, and Kate Liberman for also developing and producing Cold War Choir Practice; and to Bonnie Davis for being a fierce and dedicated advocate.

Thank you to Knud Adams for his precise, crisp, and tender vision of the play's Off-Broadway production; thank you to the cast, design team, and music team for breathing life into this wild world.

This show first came together at Brown University where it had many doulas, including Stacey Karen Robinson, the G.O.A.T. Julia Jarcho, Molly Rosa Houlahan, and Lisa D'Amour. A big thank you goes out to Aileen Wen McGroddy who directed the thesis production and a subsequent kick-ass production at Trinity Rep. I would also like to acknowledge Nicholas Pulito, Sofia Verba, and Mysia Anderson for their essential contributions to the show's early incarnations. Shout out to the Brown MFA Workshop 2022–2023!

A special thank you goes out to my family: Marc, Eric, and Karen for submitting to interviews about the late 80s; my wife, Meara Levezow, for being an incredible life partner and the play's biggest fan; Mom, AJ, and the Wisconsin aunties for trekking across the country, many many times, to support the play.

Finally, thank you to Jackie's mom for finding that weird little choir and taking us to choir practice.

Ro Reddick

Brooklyn, NY

March 2026

Cold War Choir Practice

Setting and Time

Syracuse, NY (mostly). December 1987.

Characters

Nine performers (four actors, five actor/singers)

Meek, *sharp. Not a sitcom kid. 10 years old (played by adult). Sings a bit (alto). Black.*
Smooch, **Meek**'s *dad. Former Panther; mayor of every room he walks into. 30s, Black.*
Puddin, **Meek**'s *grandma. Hawkeyed, heedful; your local Jessica Fletcher. 60s, Black.*
Clay, *Smooch's brother. Ambitious, conservative. Late 30s/early 40s, Black.*
Virgie, *Clay's wife. Ambitious, stifled, haunted. Late 30s/early 40s, white.*
The Choir, *a trio of women (expandable, if desired); diverse in age. White presenting.*

Track 1: Familiar Face (+ as cast)
Track 2: Speak + Spell (+ as cast)
Track 3: Very Good Friend (+ as cast)

Choir Leader (+ as cast), keyboardist, doubles vocals as indicated or needed.

**NOTE: You really need strong singers for this show. Between Choir Leader and The Choir you should have one alto, a strong mezzo, and two sopranos.*

Russian language script consultant: Sofia Verba.

Archival Text from President Reagan's speeches in '81 + '87 have been incorporated where indicated, courtesy of the Ronald Reagan Presidential Library.

Songs

Music + Lyrics by Ro Reddick

Happy Tidings

Milkshake for Peace

Lay Down Your Arms

Supervised Rest

The Farmer and the Businessman

Wellspring Infomercial

Star Wars

Very Good Friend

Supervised Rest Reprise

Adult Skate Night

All You Need

Virgie & The Bomb

Lay Down Your Arms Reprise

One America

A Star of Peace

THE WEIRD WORLD OF THIS PLAY *is a strange, porous space permeated by music and the iron gaze of the state.*

THE CHOIR *is a spooky organism that shapeshifts around the family. They carry the off-kilterness of the world along with its darkness. They are not neutral. They sing well (even when embodying the kids' choir).*

THE ROLLER RINK *is the center of the action, but no one is ever on actual roller skates. Skating in this play is deconstructed movement, dance – and swag.*

ADDITIONAL NOTES

[Text in brackets] is probably not spoken, if it is, it's barely heard.

– indicates that the character speaking is cut off.

/ indicates the point where the next character should speak so that their text overlaps.

Virgie is pronounced with a soft 'g' as in the state of Virginia.

Happy Tidings

Syracuse, N.Y. South Salina Street,[1] *down by the Roll-a-Rama Skating Rink. Sounds of a busy intersection: shovels scraping sidewalks, music floating from some dude's boombox.*

KKKKSSSSSSHHHH. The flipping of stations.

Boombox   Z105 Syracuse bringing you the biggest hits of '87.

Here's a new joint by Eazy-E –

KKKKSSSSSSHHHH.

Reagan Audio   At Christmas time, every home takes on a special beauty, a special warmth.[2]

KKKKSSSSSSHHHH. The radio is turned off, but is that the jingle of sleigh bells? Carolers! **The Choir** *emerges from who knows where singing. . .*

The Choir (*as carolers*)
SPECIAL, SPECIAL BEAUTY AND WARMTH AT
CHRISTMAS TIME.
SPECIAL, SPECIAL BEAUTY AND WARMTH AT
CHRISTMAS TIME.

---

[1] Pronounced [suh-LINE-uh]

[2] 'Address to the Nation About Christmas and the Situation in Poland. December 23, 1981.' The Public Papers of President Ronald W. Reagan. Ronald Reagan Presidential Library. www. reaganlibrary.gov/archives/public-papers-president-ronald-reagan (accessed December 2022).

Caroler One
DING DONG DING DONG DING
DING DING DING DING
SPECIAL BEAUTY, BEAUTY

Caroler Two
HAPPY HAPPY HAPPY TIDINGS
HAPPY HAPPY HAPPY TIDINGS
MERRY MERRY MERRY MERRY

Caroler Three
SPECIAL BEAUTY
SPECIAL WARMTH
SPECIAL WARMTH

> **Meek** *listens, sucking on an*
> *Atomic Fireball.*

The Choir (*as carolers*)
COLD COMES THE NIGHT
BUT SHELTER AND LIGHT
SHINE FROM THE GIFT WE CALL PEACE.

> **Smooch** *drags in salt for the*
> *pavement.*

Smooch   You finish shoveling that parking lot?

Meek (*re carolers*)   Dad!

Smooch   My bad.

The Choir (*as carolers*)
WARMING THE HOME, ITS BOUNDARY UNKNOWN
/ BROADENING TO ALL WHO SING

Meek
BROADENING TO ALL WHO SING

> **The Choir** *continues singing*
> *softly underneath.*

The Choir (*under dialogue*)
OOH OOH OOH
OOH OOH

Smooch   You sound good, MeekMeek.

What I tell you 'bout eating candy in the morning?

Meek   Mister Davis gave it to me –

Smooch   Give it here. Help me put this salt down.

> *The 'paper boy' tosses the day's*
> *paper to* **Smooch***. An article*
> *catches* **Smooch***'s eye.*

Meek   I finished my Christmas list.

Smooch   Whatchu making lists for? We ain't got no money.

Meek   Gran'ma said I should make a list for Santa.

Smooch   Well, Santa still owes me a new roof and a sound system, so get in line.

Meek   I want a Pound Puppy, a Speak + Spell, and a nuclear radiation detector. Dad?

Smooch (*reading*)   Ain't that some shit.

Meek   Daddy!

Smooch   What?

Meek   I want a nuclear radiation detector.

Smooch   A what now?

Meek   I want a nuclear radiation detector for my fallout shelter.

Smooch   What I tell you 'bout that fallout shelter? You been touchin my desk?

Meek   I have to put heavy stuff against the wall to protect against a nuclear blast –

Smooch   Move my desk again and Imma put a butt whoopin on that Christmas list.

Go get your stuff for choir practice.

We move to a suburb in the DMV area, our **Choir** *somehow also here, singing outside a well-appointed home.*

The Choir
HAPPY HAPPY HAPPY TIDINGS
HAPPY HAPPY HAPPY TIDINGS
HAPPY HAPPY HAPPY TIDINGS
HAPPY HAPPY HAPPY TIDINGS

Virgie *listens from inside. She is still, but just under the skin, an* *unruliness. She takes a sip of water, it calms her.*

Clay *enters with his briefcase searching the room.*

Clay   Shit. Have you seen my keys?

Virgie   You're leaving?

Clay   The president called an emergency session.

I have to go in – and of course I can't find my goddamned keys.

Virgie   Okay. Take a breath. Let me at least fix your tie.

Clay   The whole treaty could fall apart. It's a shit show – you're shaking.

Virgie   I just need to eat.

Clay   You know I wouldn't leave you alone if it weren't important.

Virgie   You have to go.

This is what we've been working towards.

All set. Did you check on top of the dresser?

Clay   Once you're better, you're next.

Virgie   I know.

Clay *runs off.*

The Choir
HAPPY TIDINGS!

The Choir *morphs into 'the group', from which a 'Familiar Face' emerges and rings the bell.*

Ding Dong

Familiar Face   Hey there, Virgie. I tried calling, but it seems you got a new number.

We've been very worried.

Virgie   You – you – you can't be here.

Familiar Face   Who says?

Clay (*off stage*)   Who's at the door?

Familiar Face   He says? Tell him, it's the Avon lady.

> **The Choir** (*as 'the group'*)
> AVON CALLING, CALLING

Virgie   It's the Avon lady.

Familiar Face   Get in the car.

Virgie   I can't go with you – I – I need –

Familiar Face   You have all you need.

> **The Choir** (*as 'the group'*)
> YOU HAVE ALL YOU NEED

Virgie   Please don't make me –

Clay (*off stage*)   You still talking to that Avon lady?

Familiar Face   Tell him, I'm stepping out for a cigarette. I'll be right back.

Virgie   I'm stepping out for a cigarette. I'll be right back.

Clay (*off stage*)   I thought you were quitting.

Familiar Face   Last one. Promise.

Virgie   Last one. Promise.

> **Virgie** *slips out the front door.*

> **The Choir** (*as 'the group'*)
> OOH OOH OOH
> OOH OOH OOH OOH
> OOH OOH OOH

All the way back at the Roll-a-Rama, **Smooch** *finishes the article, tears it out of the newspaper.*

Puddin *steps outside.*

Puddin   You got my paper?

Smooch *hands it over.*

Smooch   Meek! Let's go!

Meek *runs outside.*

Meek   Bye Gran'ma!

Puddin   Bye, baby.

The Choir (*quietly under* **Puddin**)
OOH OOH OOH
OOH OOH OOH
OOH OOH OOH OOH OOH OOH

Now what did that boy do to my paper?

Singer One
REAGONOMICS

Singer Two
COLD WAR, SOVIETS, SUPPLY SIDE, WELLSPRING

Puddin   Y'all singing carols? Y'all got some pretty voices.

Singer Three
NUCLEAR WAR, EIGHTY SEVEN, ARMAGEDDON!

Puddin (*over their singing*)	**Singer Three**	**Singer Two**	**Singer One**
Y'all might wanna find something	NUCLEAR WAR,	COLD WAR,	REA –
more positive to sing. And NO. I do	EIGHTY SEVEN,	SOVIETS,	GA –
not have any money, so don't even	ARMAGEDDON!	SUPPLY-SIDE,	NOMICS!
		WELLSPRING!	
fix ya mouth to ask. You gon' be charging	NUCLEAR WAR,	COLD WAR,	REA –
folks you need to put a little more effort	EIGHTY SEVEN,	SOVIETS,	GA –
into them lyrics – and don't fall on that ice!	ARMAGEDDON!	SUPPLY-SIDE,	NOMICS!
		WELLSPRING!	
I know ya mama don't got good insurance –	NUCLEAR WAR,	COLD WAR,	REA –
I seen her car. Don't nothin' get past	EIGHTY SEVEN,	SOVIETS,	GA –
Puddin – see now you got me lettin' all	ARMAGEDDON!	SUPPLY-SIDE,	NOMICS!
the heat out.		WELLSPRING!	

All Singers
MERRY MERRY MERRY MERRY MERRY MERRY! AH!

(*Spoken.*) Merry Christmas!

Puddin   Mm hm. Merry Christmas.

> *Inside the Roll-a-Rama,* **Puddin**
> *flips through channels stopping*
> *on PBS. (Rolls right into next*
> *scene . . .)*

Milkshake For Peace

The Roll-a-Rama television.

PBS Announcer   We hope you're enjoying 'Give Us Peace!: A Concert at the United Nations', featuring The Seedlings of Peace, one of the premiere children's choirs in the country with local chapters in fifteen states. Programming like this is made possible by members like you.

> **The Choir** *embodies the theatrical concert performers.* '**Parent**' *brings a milkshake to* '**American Child**'.

Parent   What's the matter, Jane?

American Child   I'm feeling kinda down, what with the threat of nuclear war and all.

Parent   I bet this milkshake will cheer you up.

American Child   I'd like to share a milkshake with a Soviet friend.

Parent   They don't have milkshakes in the Soviet Union, you can only get that in America, where we're free.

Maybe someday it will be different and you can share that milkshake with a Soviet friend.

American Child   I want a Soviet friend now!

> *And just like that an actual* **Soviet Child** *appears via satellite. The* **American Child** *lifts their milkshake towards the screen and it pops (magically!) into frame with the* **Soviet Child**.

American Child
I GIVE MY DRINK TO A SOVIET CHILD.
I LET HER SIP FROM MY STRAW.
AND THEN WE TALK OF OUR DIFFERENCES

AND WE DISCOVER THEY ARE SMALL.
NO ONE HAS TO DIE

All
NO ONE HAS TO DIE.
MILKSHAKE FOR A SOVIET AND I
NO ONE HAS TO DIE, NO ONE HAS TO DIE.
MILKSHAKE FOR A SOVIET AND I

American Child
I HAVE GROWN CLOSE TO THIS SOVIET CHILD

Soviet Child
BEST FRIEND

American Child
WE LIKE TO BRUSH EACH OTHER'S HAIR

Societ Child
'TIL THE END

American Child
I TEACH HER WORDS LIKE 'FREEDOM', 'PEACE'

All
AND SANCTION

American Child
THEN WE SING A PRAYER: NO ONE HAS TO DIE

American & Soviet Child	**Parent**
NO ONE HAS TO DIE.	(. . . MILKSHAKE FOR)
NO ONE HAS TO DIE	
MILKSHAKE FOR A	
SOVIET	
A SOVIET AND I – DON'T	A SOVIET AND I – DON'T
DIE!	DIE!
NO ONE HAS TO DIE!	NO ONE HAS TO DIE!

Soviet Child (*spoken*)
Freedom. Peace. Milkshake.

All
MILKSHAKE FOR A SOVIET AND I!

> **Puddin** *turns off the TV, but the music continues, this time from a keyboard across town (rolls right into next scene. . .)*

Lay Down Your Arms

Rehearsal for the local Seedlings
of Peace chapter.

Children's Choir
NO ONE HAS TO DIE, NO ONE HAS TO DIE!
MILKSHAKE FOR A SOVIET AND I! –

Choir Leader   Okay. I'm nervous. Our Public Access concert is coming up and you sound . . . hollow. No one's gonna tell you this because you're so young – I don't even know how old you are – Jackie, what are you, like, five? You're seven? You're very small – No one's gonna tell you this, but right now the Soviets have over 40,000 nuclear warheads: ballistic missiles, MIG 21s, MIG 23s – I'm not trying to scare you, I just want you to know what we're dealing with.

You know, I was there. In Moscow, in eighty-five, at the first Seedlings of Peace concert. I was the one who went on a smoke break in the Red Square and spotted, Ludmila, standing under the banner of Gorbachev. I ran to her, brushed the home-cut bangs from her eyes, and implored her to sing with us as an authentic Soviet child. She sang with something none of you have: an unshakeable faith that the voice of a child can stop a nuclear attack. You should all be Ludmila. I got you something I think will help . . .

(*Pulls out index cards.*) Soviet pen pals! There's one for each of you. Close your eyes. Picture the majestic Ural Mountains. Zoom in real close. Do you see her? Little Ludmila? She's up on her tippy toes waving. Sing to her. Teach her about freedom in the west.

Meek begins a letter.

Meek   Dear Soviet Pen Pal,

War is imminent. How are you today? Did you know the voice of a child has the power to stop a nuclear attack? Choir Leader told us that, so I thought I'd share it in case it's useful. A kid from choir said I don't have to worry about getting bombed in my neighborhood because / only Black people live there and they always bomb important people first.

Kid From Choir (*a reassurance*) . . . only Black people live there and they always bomb important people first.

Meek   But my dad said / I don't know why you worried 'bout them Russians.

Smooch   I don't know why you worried 'bout them Russians.

The FBI just bombed a bunch of Black folks in Philly.

Meek   But, I'm building a fallout shelter in my dad's office just in case. I still need a nuclear radiation detector. It's on my Christmas list along with a Pound Puppy and a Speak + Spell. Do you have a fallout shelter? My dad runs the Roll-a-Rama on South Salina Street. We live above it with my gran'ma. Where do you live? Moscow? Is that near the Ural Mountains? It's very snowy in Syracuse. You would feel at home. Does your dad make you shovel?

Your American Pen Pal,

Meek.

Choir practice continues.

Soloist	**Children's Choir + Meek**
I'M JUST A CHILD	. . .
WHO STANDS BEFORE	
YOU	(. . . JUST A CHILD)
MY ONLY POWER	. . .
IS TO SING MY SONG	(. . . SING MY SONG)

MISTER PRESIDENT!   (PRESIDENT!)
MISTER GORBACHEV!   (GORBACHEV!)
MISTER PRESIDENT!   (PRESIDENT!)
MISTER GORBACHEV!   (GORBACHEV!)

All
GOR-BA-CHEV!

Soloist
LAY DOWN YOUR. . .

All
ARMS

Choir Leader   Much better. I'll see you all next week.

> **Smooch** *emerges from the swirl*
> *of kids and parents.*

Smooch   MeekMeek! Over here! That was nice. Very very nice.

(*To the parents and kids.*) Excuse me! Uh, excuse me everyone. Hi. I'm Meek's dad. You can call me Smooch. I run the Roll-a-Rama over on the south side. And, uh – you all sound beautiful by the way. Everybody needs to see this. Young folks singing about peace. 'Cause these mo'fuckas out here – excuse my French. You know, I noticed you all be singing in French –

Meek   Russian –

Smooch   Okay, well, I noticed you all got a lotta songs in French – Russian, whatever, and you got a lotta songs about a little Soviet Child, and a little this and that child. And I think you need a song or two about a little Black child, 'cause we at war now too, okay. We got the FBI bombin' folks – we got the pigs out in our neighborhoods – Now you got me started see –

Meek   Dad, please –

Smooch   And you think I ain't notice Meek the only one of us up in this little choir? PSSHHH up in here beggin': 'Mister president, please. Please mister president' – what kind of song is that? You need to be *tellin* that mo'fucka: 'We want freedom. We want employment. We want education' – That's three lyrics right there, got seven more ready to go –

Meek   Dad!

Smooch   Okay, see now, that's not even what I was gonna say. Uh, anyway . . .

I would like to invite you all down to the Roll-a-Rama this weekend for some skatin'. And I'll throw in a coupon for some free fries. Alright? No, no, my pleasure. But that coupon is for regular fries. You want disco fries, you gotta ask ya mama. That shit ain't free. Alright? Alright. Power to the people.

Supervised Rest

> *A clinic for a very particular kind of recovery. A* **Caring Professional** *peruses* **Virgie***'s chart.*

Clay   She stepped out for a smoke and disappeared. The guy who runs the gas station by the highway found her wandering around.

Caring Professional   Virgie, can you tell us where you were?

Virgie   . . .

Caring Professional   Did someone make you leave?

> **Virgie** *is completely lost in the soft intoning of 'the group' that only she can hear.*
>
> **The Choir** (*as 'the group'*)
> OOH OOH OOH

Virgie   . . .

Caring Professional   How long has she been non-responsive?

Clay   Since they found her. She was finally making progress . . . If this is Wellspring –

    The Choir (*as 'the group'*)
    OOH OOH OOH

Caring Professional   We don't know if it's Wellspring, a number of things could've triggered her, left her in a state of shock.

Clay   But if it *is* . . . I don't think I can do this again.

Caring Professional   Let's focus on Virgie's care. Is she hydrating?

Clay   She won't drink.

Caring Professional   She needs to hydrate. It will help her reset. And she needs rest – supervised, of course, and, preferably, at home. Are you able to stay with her?

Clay   . . . You understand my work? What I do?

Caring Professional   Yes, of course –

Clay   Then you know that's just not possible.

Caring Professional   Perhaps her family –

Clay   That's me. It's just me.

Caring Professional   If this is the group, she needs to be someplace where they can't get to her. Do you have any family outside the city?

Virgie coughs.

Clay   It's okay, hon. I'll get you some water.

The Choir (*as 'the group'*)
LA LA   LA LA   LA LA   LA
LA LA LA LA
LA LA LA LA LA LA
LA LA L A
LA LA LA LA
LA LA   LA LA   LA LA
LA LA LA LA LA

Pig Feet Through the Phone

> *Roll-a-Rama. School's out.* **Meek**
> *cuts across the skating rink.* `

Meek   Hey, Daddy!

Smooch   Hey baby, how was school?

Meek (*going going gone*)   Good!

Smooch (*calling after her*)   What I tell you 'bout runnin'
inside . . .

> *In comes* **Puddin**.

Puddin   Mailman come?

Smooch   Probably. Let me show you somethin' real quick?

> **Smooch** *hands her a stack of
> coupons.*

Smooch   I had Herc make these up.

Puddin   What we need coupons for?

Smooch   I gave some out at Meek's choir practice – they ate
it up! We get that north side money during the day, use it for
Adult Skate Night in the evenin' – BAM. This place gonna be
the spot again.

Puddin   From a coupon?

Smooch   Just anybody come through, give 'em one of these.

Puddin   Mmm hmm.

> **Puddin** *goes off to get the mail.*
>
> **Meek** *cuts through with an
> armful of used two liter soda
> bottles, rinsed and filled with tap
> water.*

Meek   Daddy, can I have the keys to the office?

Smooch   Whatchu doin with them bottles?

Meek   It's water. For my emergency kit.

Smooch (*tossing keys*)   Betta not let your grandmother see that.

Meek   Thanks, Daddy!

The phone rings.

Smooch   Roll-a-Rama Skating where there ain't no party like a Roll-a-Rama party 'cause a Roll-a-Rama party don't stop. How may I help you?

. . . Who dis?

. . . Nah nigga.

Smooch *hangs up.*

The phone rings again. **Smooch** *hangs it up immediately.*

It rings again. He hangs it up, then lifts the receiver off the hook.

Puddin *comes back with the mail and a package.*

Puddin   Who was that on the phone?

Smooch   Nobody.

Puddin   Meek! You got a package!

Meek (*off stage*)   What?!

Puddin   A package!

Meek *runs in.*

Smooch   Who you got sendin' packages?

Meek   I don't know. What is it?

Puddin   Open it up.

Meek *opens the package.*

Smooch (*re the note attached*)   Let me see that.

Meek   It's a Speak + Spell!

Smooch (*reads the card*)   'For Meeksnaya. Merry Christmas.' Who the hell is Meeksnaya?

Meek   It's from my Soviet pen pal!

Smooch   A who? –

Meek   My Soviet pen pal –

Puddin   From that little choir / she in.

Smooch   Nah, nah, nah you gotta send that back. / I ain't got no money for that.

Meek   But it's a Christmas gift! It's free! / Please, Dad!

Puddin   Let her keep the toy, Smooch.

Smooch   Okay. But your little friend betta not come up in here with a bill.

Meek   Thank you, Daddy!

Puddin *notices the phone off the hook and returns it.*

It rings almost immediately.

Puddin   Roll-a-Rama Skating where there ain't no party like a Roll-a-Rama party 'cause a Roll-a-Rama party don't stop. This is Puddin . . . Clay is that you?

Smooch   [Hang up. Hang up.]

Puddin   You sound good, Clay. Like you livin high on the hog. I can almost smell the pig feet through the phone. You still eat pig feet, Clay?

Smooch   That nigga ain't eatin no pig feet.

Puddin   How's political life? I see them white folks ain't run you out they party yet. Give 'em time. So what's wrong, 'cause you don't ever call ya mama no more. Something must be up.

. . . Mmm hmm . . . mmm.

. . . Okay, but you know ya mama always finds out.

. . . Smooch?

Smooch   [Nope.]

Puddin   Smooch ain't here.

. . . Well, you know I wanna see ya, but ya brotha's a different story.

. . . Okay, come on up –

Smooch   / [No no no.]

Puddin (*hanging up*)   We'll see ya Saturday, Clay.

> *Still nestled in a corner,* **Meek** *turns on the Speak + Spell. We hear its three toned melody.*
>
> **The Choir**
> AH AH AH!
>
> **Meek** *begins a letter.*

Meek   Dear Soviet Pen Pal,

Thank you for my Speak + Spell! I love it! I don't have money to buy you a present, but our roller rink is next door to Davis's Candy Emporium. Mr. Davis gives me Atomic Fireballs for shoveling out his entrance. I'm gonna put one in with this letter. Dad said not to put nice stuff through the post office because / they be stealin' people's mail . . .

> **Smooch**   They be stealin' people's mail if they think something good is in it.

Meek   But you can't be mad/ 'cause the government don't be paying people enough.

> **Smooch**   'Cause the government don't be payin' people enough.

Meek   So you might not get it. I wonder how long this will take to reach you? Choir Leader says / a long range intercontinental ballistic missile. . .

> **Choir Leader**   A long range intercontinental ballistic missile takes only thirty minutes to reach the United States from the Soviet Union.

Meek   That's why our concerts are exactly twenty-eight minutes long. / Just in case . . .

> **Choir Leader**   Just in case a missile launches when we start.

Meek   We'd still have two minutes to hug our families before we die.

Gran'ma says / two minutes ain't gonna make no difference . . .

> **Puddin**   Two minutes ain't gonna make no difference, so you might as well use the whole thirty.

Meek   Does your dad let people visit you? I could come and teach you some songs. Maybe they work better if we sing 'em from there. Write me when you get this! I want to know if you got the fireball!

Your American Pen Pal,

Meek.

Chicken Dance

KKRRRRRRRSSSSHHH

The aging sound system creaks to life.

A familiar polka cranks up, chirping a major key safe for mom and dad and kid and babe.

Reagan Audio   Just as truth can flourish only when the journalist is given freedom of speech.

Prosperity can come about only when the farmer and businessman enjoy economic freedom.[3]

A tsunami of alabaster children eat through the doors. Roaring with giggles. Dripping snot and handmade mittens.

Heads thrown fore and aft with a violent gnashing; the raw sewage of Baby Ruth, cherry coke, and fart jokes, swirl along their tongues.

How they laugh! (How it jangles the nerves.)

Now for the chicken dance. The eerily synced flapping of 'chicken

---

[3] 'Remarks on East-West Relations at the Brandenburg Gate in West Berlin June 12, 1987.' The Public Papers of President Ronald W. Reagan. Ronald Reagan Presidential Library. www.reaganlibrary.gov/archives/public-papers-president-ronald-reagan (accessed December 2022).

wings' and shaking of 'chicken butts'.

** CLAP * CLAP * CLAP * CLAP **

Now the churn. A messy stirring, round and round, agitating the wax on **Puddin**'s *freshly cleaned floor.*

It's Saturday afternoon at the Roll-a-Rama skating rink!

It's Good To Be Home

> **Smooch** *gets on the mic.*

Smooch   Hello everyone. Thank you you all for coming out. It's a different crowd for us – but don't be afraid to come back! Matter fact, we havin' Adult Skate Night later on tonight. You can tuck the kids into bed, change out of them khakis, and I'll show you how we get down on the south side. Alright. I thought it'd be nice to have the choir give us a sneak peek of they concert. Give it up for the Seedlings of Peace!

> *Applause. The* **Choir Leader** *gets* **Meek** *and the other 'seedlings' into formation.*

Children's Choir + Meek
THE FARMER AND THE BUSINESS MAN
PROSPER IN THE WEST.
THE FARMER PROSPERS WHEN HIS
BUSINESS CAN PROGRESS.
THE HARVEST OF PROSPERITY TRICKLES DOWN
LIKE
RAIN ON LEAVES.
THE FARMER AND THE BUSINESSMAN
PROSPER IN THE WEST.

> *The skating music starts back up and the children return to skating.* **Clay** *leads* **Virgie** *in.*

Puddin   Hey, stranger!

Clay   Hi, Ma.

Puddin   Smooch! MeekMeek! Look who's here!

> **Puddin**, **Smooch**, **Meek**, **Clay**, *and* **Virgie** *squish together in a banquette.* **Virgie***'s still not quite with it.*

Puddin   It's good to finally spend time with you both.

Clay   It's good to be home.

Puddin   We haven't seen you since the wedding.

Course we were sitting so far back, hardly felt like we were there at all.

Clay   You weren't that far back, Ma.

Puddin   Weren't that close neither.

Smooch   You can set your briefcase down. Ain't nobody gonna take it.

Clay   It's for work. I can't afford to misplace it.

Meek (*off* **Virgie**)   That lady dead?

Smooch   She ain't dead.

Clay   This is your Aunt Virgie, remember?

Puddin   She don't look too good.

Clay   She's okay. She's just tired.

Puddin (*to* **Virgie**)   You want some food, honey?

Virgie   . . .

Smooch   She don't speak?

Clay   She's tired.

Puddin   Must be. That was a long drive.

Virgie *coughs*.

Clay   And dehydrated.

Puddin   Bring her some water, Meek.

Clay   / Thank you.

Smooch   Nah nah. Meek sit down. Don't be ordering my child around.

Clay   I wasn't ordering anyone around –

Puddin   It's just a glass of water. Meek, go'n and get your /
auntie some water.

Smooch   She ain't the help! Sit down, Meek –

Clay   / Who said she was the help?

Puddin   Ain't nobody called that child the help.

Smooch   You got her runnin', fetchin' water / like she work
for you.

Clay   I didn't ask her for anything –

Puddin   I'll get the damn water –

Smooch   No, Ma! You got a bad back!

Puddin   / I can lift a glass of water! –

Clay   It's a glass of water! –

Smooch   I don't care!

Clay   I will go get water for my wife!

Smooch   Who you raisin' your voice at?

Clay   Whoever I damn well please –

Smooch   I know you better take that bass outcha voice –

Clay   Or what? / I'm not afraid of you.

Smooch   Oh you tryin' to flex? –

Puddin   I don't want no fightin'! I said I would get the
water! –

Smooch   If she thirsty she can get her own damn water!

> **Meek** *sets down a glass of water.*
> *Silence.*

Smooch   Meek, sit down.

(*To* **Virgie**.) 'Thank you' is customary.

Puddin   Don't start, Smooch. You see that child ain't well.

Clay   Please try, hon. You have to hydrate.

> **Virgie** *forces the water down. It helps.*

Virgie *coughs.*

Puddin   You want another water, honey?

Virgie *nods.*

> **Puddin** *nods to* **Meek***, who gets another glass.*

Puddin   I was pretty worried when you called. I didn't know if Virgie was sick or hurt or what?

Clay   She's just tired.

Puddin   You keep sayin' that –

Clay   Because it's true –

Puddin   But she don't seem her normal self. Don't have that pep.

Smooch   Yeah, what happened to that pep, Clay?

Clay   She had some trouble and that took a lot out of her. And now she needs rest.

Puddin   What kind of trouble?

Smooch   Yeah, what kind of trouble, Clay?

Clay   Nothing to worry over. She, uh, she attended some workshops that help professionals achieve optimal productivity and –

Smooch   She don't look too optimal to me.

Clay   That's why we're here. She pushed herself too hard.

I thought a visit with family might be restful.

Meek *brings water.* **Virgie**
drinks it, signals for another.

Puddin (*to* **Virgie**)   At least your skin won't ash up drinkin'
all that water.

Smooch   So you drove her six hours to come here and rest?

Clay   She wants to spend Christmas with the family.

Puddin   Christmas is three weeks away.

Smooch   Which family you stayin' with?

Clay   / With you obviously –

Puddin   They stayin' with us.

Smooch   They ain't stayin' here. You betta find a hotel or
something –

Puddin   They not stayin' at a hotel! / They family!

Clay   Virgie can't stay at a hotel.

Smooch   They got some nice ones downtown. Bring you
water all day long –

Puddin   They are not stayin' at a hotel!

Clay   Virgie has to stay with Ma.

Smooch   Ma live wit' me. So where y'all stayin'?

Puddin   / Come on now, Smooch.

Clay   She can't be alone. She needs to stay here with Ma.

Puddin   You not stayin', Clay?

Meek *brings water.* **Virgie**
downs it. The fog is slowly lifting.

Clay   There's a summit at the White House next week. We
finally got a treaty hammered out with the Soviets – I really
shouldn't even be talking to you about this –

Smooch   Nigga, you ain't big time –

Clay   Oh! That's not big time? / Nuclear disarmament? This is not a game. Ma?

Smooch   Nope. Nope. Nope.

Puddin   Smooch, let your brother talk.

Clay   We thought we had a deal on the treaty, but now Gorbachev is threatening to pull out.

I'm assuming you know who Gorbachev is –

Smooch   / This nigga . . .

Meek   I know who that is! We sing a song to him in my choir. For peace.

Clay   That's very sweet. But grown ups, like your uncle, are working really hard to make sure the Soviets don't blow up your daddy's roller rink.

Puddin   Don't say stuff like that to that child –

Smooch   Maybe I like the Soviets. Least they thinkin 'bout the working man –

Clay   You are so ignorant! –

Puddin   Come on, now, you two!

(*To* **Clay**.) I don't understand, y'all leavin or stayin?

Clay   I have to get back to D.C. and, uh, Virgie needs. . . supervision.

Smooch   OH! HO HO! This negro here!

So you brought your **parched ass wife** to my house for me to babysit?!

Clay   Watch what you say about my wife!

Puddin   She is drinkin' a lot of water, Clay.

Smooch   After you was bad mouthin' us in the New York Times!

Clay   That's what this is about? / That's why you're mad?

Puddin   What's that now? –

Smooch   See, I wasn't gonna say nuttin' 'cause of Ma – but fuck it. You up in here tryin' to flex –

Puddin   What was in the Times?

Clay   It's nothing, Ma. Just press for my new job.

Smooch   Yeah, he ain't tell you 'bout that interview, huh ma? / Tryin' to be the big man up in the White House.

Clay   Why are you always stirring shit up?

Puddin   You didn't tell me you was in the paper, Clay –

Clay   'Cause it's nothing –

Smooch   He was in the paper alright. Talkin' 'bout how when he was growin' up his family was 'hooked on welfare'.

Puddin   Clay, I know you didn't say nothin' like that.

Smooch   That's a direct quote. From Mister Deputy National Security Advisor himself.

> **Smooch** *pulls out the newspaper clipping from earlier.*

Smooch   I got it right here. . .

(*Reading.*) 'I am ashamed to say I watched my family celebrate government checks like a kid on Christmas. Reagan finally gave Black folks a chance to build something for ourselves.'

Puddin   Let me see that.

> **Puddin** *reads in this long tense silence.*

Virgie   May I have another?

Puddin   That's enough of that! So which hotel she stayin' at?

Clay   Please, Ma. Ma?

Puddin's *gone with* **Smooch** *right behind her.* **Meek** *hangs back, unnoticed.*

Clay   Dammit.

. . . Hey, hon? Hey? How are you feeling?

Virgie   I, uh . . . I don't know.

Clay   That's okay, it's okay. You're going to rest here with Ma / and I'm going to head back home –

Virgie   What? –You're leaving me? – No –

Clay   Ma's going to look after you –

Virgie   I want to come home with you –

Clay   I need you to stay here.

Virgie   I don't feel comfortable here, Clay.

Clay   You know I wouldn't go if I didn't have to. I'll come back to get you –

Virgie   When?

Clay   When you're better. Promise.

(*Wrapping her up.*) I love you. I'll bring your bags in from the car.

Clay *takes his briefcase and leaves.*

The rink's in that dead zone before Adult Skate Night. **Meek** *gives* **Virgie** *the remote to the TV.*

Still shaky, **Virgie** *turns it on and flips through stations. She stops on an infomercial, a Wellspring Women's Optimization Workshop.*

> *That soft drone returns.* **Virgie** *is somehow there and not there, viewer 'at home' and workshop participant.*

Familiar Face (*as Workshop Leader* (*on the TV*))   That's because our work is based in science. So we know the tools work. Why don't you start by sharing a challenge you're having at work.

Young Woman (*on TV*)	**Virgie**
Well, uh, I like my job, but I'm the only woman	. . .
	I'm the only woman.
And it's been hard.	. . .
	It has been hard.

Familiar Face (*as Workshop Leader*)   Well, work is hard – for everyone, right?

Young Woman	**Virgie**
I don't know.	I don't know.
	My husband's doing so well and
. . .	
I feel stuck	I feel stuck.

Familiar Face (*as Workshop Leader*)   I wonder if this isn't an optimization problem in disguise. What's the first tool we use in our work?

Young Woman	**Virgie**
Feedback loops.	Feedback loops.

Familiar Face (*as Workshop Leader*)   Good. They tell you how you're showing up for the group, helping the group progress, not draining it. And you can do all of this for the group because . . .?

Young Woman   I'm not sure.

Familiar Face (*as Workshop Leader*)   You have all you need.

Applause.

Familiar Face (*as Workshop Leader*)   Say it.

Young Woman	**Virgie**
I have all I –	I –

> **Virgie** *turns the television off, but the voices of the group still haunt her . . .*
>
> **The Choir** (*as 'the group'*) ALL YOU NEED. YOU HAVE ALL YOU –

Virgie   No. Come on, Virgie. You don't need that. Get yourself together, so you can go home!

Easy easy easy. You're calm. You can do this.

(*A rehearsal.*)   Clay, I'm feeling exuberant. No. Shit.

I'm feeling excellent – like myself – please take me home.

Clay, I'm feeling so much better now –

Puddin   Clay's outside.

Virgie   I know. I'm feeling so much better now.

Puddin   I heard. You want some disco fries or something?

Virgie   No, thank you, I'm sure we'll be leaving soon.

Puddin   Might be a while. Smooch took the air out of Clay's tires. They out there fightin' 'bout that now.

You do seem a little better. Clay said those workshops you was in really took it out of you.

What kind of stuff they had y'all doin'?

Virgie   Just productivity exercises.

Puddin   Clay said you was working real hard, tryin' to get 'optimal'. Whatever that means.

Virgie   It's just a way to succeed in business and in life.

Puddin   I need to sign Smooch up for one of them workshops. Who's runnin' it again?

Virgie   No one you would've heard of. Just a group in D.C. But it's – it's very selective, so . . .

Puddin   Oh, okay. You making moves, Virgie. Clay's like that too. I see why y'all together. I'm glad he got you. It's hard out there for him.

Virgie   It's hard for him – and it's hard for me too. But we don't focus on that. We push each other.

Puddin   To get optimal?

Virgie   You could say that.

Puddin   Just be careful. My cousin Shirley's son went to a workshop at the Marriott, dropped his whole paycheck on some wheat grass and a bag of crystals. Ain't been right since.

Virgie   I'd better find Clay. Let him know I'm feeling better –

Puddin   I'll go get him for ya'. You stay right there. Don't you move, now. Meek. Come here.

Puddin pulls Meek to the side.

Puddin   I gotta go see about your uncle. I want you to keep an eye her. Something 'bout that woman ain't right – and make sure she stay out of my kitchen, drinking up all my water like she ain't got no sense – she know good and god damn well water ain't free – see that's how rich folks do, they show they ass, and then they look at you like *you* wasn't raised right. I swear to god, Meek, she look at you sideways, you betta tell me, she try to get in my water again, tell me – matter fact, she use the toilet, I wanna report on what she put in it. 'Cause see your uncle think I was born two minutes past yesterday – actin brand new in the newspaper 'cause he got a job at the White House. Keeping secrets like we ain't kin. Bringing that spooky looking woman up in here! Let me find out she in one of them cults! Now what ya uncle don't know is, Puddin's on high alert! Don't let her out of your sight, Meek – you got that?

Meek   Got it.

Puddin   Good.

> **Puddin** *leaves.* **Meek** *watches*
> **Virgie**'s *every move.*

Virgie   Please stop staring at me. It's unnerving.

Meek   Gran'ma told me to watch you. She told me to watch you so you don't drink anymore of her water.

Virgie   I don't want anymore of her water –

Meek   Good. 'Cause you can't have it. You rich?

Virgie   Your uncle and I work very hard.

Meek   Gran'ma said rich folks wasn't raised right, that's why you drinkin' up all her water even though you know good and god damn well water ain't free.

Virgie   You shouldn't curse.

Meek   You gonna pee the bed you keep doin' that.

Virgie   I've never done that.

Meek   Liar. You in a cult?

Virgie   No.

Meek   Liar.

Virgie   I'm not in a cult. I was in a group. It made me very tired, but I'm feeling much better now.

Meek   Uncle Clay in a cult?

Virgie   No.

Meek   He pee the bed like you?

Virgie   I do not 'pee the bed'! Can you please go skate with your friends or something?

Meek   They left – and they're not my friends. We just sing in a choir together. Why your face look like that?

Virgie   Because my head hurts, because you keep talking to me. Please stop.

> **Meek** *turns on the* **Speak + Spell**.
>
> **The Choir**
> AH AH AH!

Speak + Spell   Speak and Spell. Spell: Privet.

> **Meek** *types it in.*

Speak + Spell   That is correct! Spell: Gosundarstvennyy Chinovnik.

> **Meek** *types it in.*

Speak + Spell   That is correct! Molodets! Tak derzhat!

Meek   Molodets! Tak derzhat!

Virgie   What is that?

Meek   It's my Speak + Spell.

Virgie   Those words are very unusual.

Speak + Spell   Spell: Revolyutsiya.

Meek (*typing*)   Revolyutsiya. It's Russian.

Virgie   May I see that?

Meek   No.

Virgie   Where did you get that?

Meek   From my Soviet pen pal.

Virgie   Where did you get a Soviet pen pal?

Meek Choir Leader gave us pen pals.

Virgie The Soviets are our enemies. You cannot be pen pals.

Meek Can too! We're going to go deep in the bosom of the Ural Mountains, then I'm gonna teach her how to build a fallout shelter, then we're gonna use our voices to stop the atomic bomb. You're welcome. Do you even have a plan?

Virgie For what?

Meek Nuclear war.

Virgie No, I don't have a plan.

Meek So you're just going to perish?

Virgie You're too young for such dark thoughts.

Meek No, I'm not.

Virgie You are. You should be playing with American toys and focusing on school.

Meek After Armageddon there won't be any schools. Our toys will be the bones of the dead, slick with blood and warm with radiation.

Virgie Did your toy teach you that word? Armageddon?

Meek A kid in my choir went to Russia on exchange.

She said her host family was / so poor they didn't even have a washer or dryer. . .

> **Kid From Choir** . . . so poor, they didn't even have a washer or dryer.
>
> I had to wash my jeans by hand in the kitchen sink, then hang them out of the window to dry!

Meek   I told her that we don't have a dryer at home and that I hang my clothes on the line in the pantry.

She said, / 'You won't have to do that . . .'

> **Kid From Choir**   You won't have to do that . . . / after Armageddon . . .
>
> **The Choir/Meek**   After Armageddon. . .
>
> **The Choir**
> IN THE FINAL FRONTIER
> . . .

Meek   She said / that's why she went to Russia . . .

> **Kid From Choir**   That's why I went to Russia. I wanted to see it before we nuked it.
>
> **The Choir**
> STARS AND MOONS DISAPPEAR.

Meek   Or they nuke us. She said / the president is building a soccer net in space. . .

> **Kid From Choir**   The president is building a soccer net in space to catch nukes before they hit New York.
>
> He calls it Star Wars, but the Soviets are onto him, and they're gonna try and nuke us before it's finished.
>
> **Choir**
> 'CROSS THE MILKY WAY, NUCLEAR ATTACK

CATCH IT IN A NET, TOSS IT BACK

Virgie   That's not going to happen.

Meek   How do you know?

Virgie   Your uncle's been working very hard with the president to protect us. It's not going to happen.

Meek   How do you know that?

Virgie   The whole world knows that. That's why the world's in sync with us economically, politically. Because we win.

Meek   But how?

Virgie   The president is very smart. He knows what the Soviets are going to do before they do it. He has a network of spies. Razor thin men who disappear into cracks. They have no chins or cheeks, only eyes and ears and tips of fingers. They can crack open the mind of the Soviet, slip inside, and steal their secrets.

Meek   The mind is a private thing.

Virgie   There are no private things. And it's not a soccer net. It's a series of satellites that will blanket the globe like snow on Christmas morning.

> **Virgie** *starts to leave.*

Meek   Where are you going?

Virgie   To the bathroom. Do not even think of following me.

> **Meek** *is alone.*

Speak + Spell   Spell: Pasport

> **Meek** *types it in.*

Speak + Spell   That is correct! Vashi dokumenty?

> **Meek** *types it in.*

Speak + Spell   That is incorrect. Vashi dokumenty?

Meek   Do you have your travel documents.

Speak + Spell   Da ili net, Meeksnaya? Please answer. Are you there?

Meek   Yes.

Speak + Spell   Do you have your travel documents? Yes or no?

Meek   I don't know. Who are you?

Speak + Spell   I am your friend, Meeksnaya.

Meek   Are you my Soviet pen pal?

Speak + Spell   Yes, I am your Soviet pen pal.

Meek   How are you talking to me?

Speak + Spell   It is like phone. I am calling you from very far away.

Meek   Are you in Russia?

Speak + Spell   Yes, I am deep in the bosom of the Ural Mountains.

Meek   Wow. What is it like there?

Speak + Spell   It is beautiful, Meeksnaya. There are horses and flowing rivers. Each day I wear warm sweaters and eat sweet cakes and sing at the top of the mountain.

Meek   Did you ask your dad if I can come visit?

Speak + Spell   Yes, Meeksnaya. He would love for you to come. You will not want to leave.

Meek   But aren't you afraid?

Speak + Spell   Of what, Meeksnaya?

Meek   Of not having any friends. Aunt Virgie said that the whole world is in sync, except for the Soviet Union. Doesn't that mean you don't have friends?

Speak + Spell   The Soviet Union has many friends.

Meek   I don't have any friends.

Speak + Spell   You have me, Meeksnaya. And friends make you strong. I am so happy we are friends.

Meek   I'm happy we're friends, too. You got a washing machine? Are you rich or poor?

Speak + Spell   We are not rich, but everyone has land, bread, justice, and peace.

Meek   My dad says that's how it should be!

Speak + Spell   Ah, your dad would make very good comrade. You should bring him! He would like Russia very much.

Meek   Are there Black people in Russia?

Speak + Spell   . . .

Meek   Hello?

Speak + Spell   There are some. You would not be alone. Do you trust your Soviet pen pal, Meeksnaya?

Meek   Yes.

Speak + Spell   Kharasho. What if I told you, Mother Russia will give you what you most desire, if you give something to Mother Russia.

Meek   Like what?

Speak + Spell   I have a friend, a very good friend. She wants to meet you. She will tell you what it is you can do for Mother Russia. And if you agree, you will come and live in peace in Ural Mountains with your family.

Meek   Really?

Speak + Spell   Yes, Meeksnaya. It will be so nice. Will you meet my Very Good Friend?

Meek   Where?

Speak + Spell   A secret place. You must come alone. You cannot tell anyone. Will you meet my Very Good Friend?

Meek   I don't know –

Speak + Spell   There is not much time. Will you meet –

> **Meek** *turns off the* **Speak + Spell**.

A Little Question Mark

Outside the Roll-a-Rama. **Clay** *tries to go back inside.*

Clay   Unlock the door.

Smooch   Sorry. Closed til eight –

Clay   I need to call Triple A –

Smooch   Not on my phone!

Clay   I don't fucking believe this. / Open the door!

Smooch   Believe that shit! . . . Nope.

Puddin   That's enough! Smooch, go inside and cool off.

Smooch goes inside.

Clay   Did you see what he did to my car?!

Puddin   We'll get somebody to look at it.

Clay   I'm using the fucking phone! –

Puddin   Let him cool off for a minute. You need to cool off too.

Clay   I quite literally do not have time for this!

Puddin   Give it a minute, Clay.

Smooch *comes out carrying two telephones in his hand.*

Puddin   What are you doin'?

Smooch   Goin' to the store.

Puddin   Why you takin' the phones to the store, Smooch?

Smooch   He ain't using my shit.

Clay   You are so small, man! –

Smooch   So then take yo ass home –

Clay   I'M TRYING!

Smooch   Ma, I swear to god, when I come back I betta not find him in my rink.

> **Smooch** *leaves.* **Meek** *stands in the doorway unseen.*

Clay   I don't want to be in your goddamn rink! Am I crazy??? Am I going crazy??? Because I'm averting a NUCLEAR DISASTER – but oh! Never mind that! Never mind that! – Because Smooch is mad – Smooch is mad so the entire world has to fucking stop while he pouts! It's bullshit, Ma and you know it!

Puddin (*after a moment*)   You done?

Your brother got a right to be mad. Me too for that matter. What you said really hurt.

Clay   I didn't mean to hurt you, Ma.

Puddin   But did you mean what you said?

Clay   I'm in these rooms now, Ma. Big rooms. With the secretary of state, secretary of defense – and I got the president, Ma, the president asking for me by name. The world's falling apart and these men get to sit down and figure out how to save it – and I'm right there with them. But do you know, the whole time I'm sitting there, the only thing I can think about is that little question mark that pops up right there, right on the brow of every man in that room as soon as I open my mouth, asking, 'Who left the side door open? Who let that negro slip through?' I need them to know where I stand. What kind of man I am. So, yeah, I meant what I said.

Puddin   Well, you got some kind of memory. I'll tell you that. What you remember as celebratin', I remember as relief. The kind of relief that kept your belly full and got you off to school each morning, so you can be in one of them big rooms. . . 'hooked' – I call that need, but you do what you gotta do.

You show them folks what kind of man you are. Just know, you showin me too.

Clay   . . .

Puddin   . . .

Clay   That phone booth still around the corner?

Puddin   Yeah, but it don't work. Don't hardly none of 'em work.

Clay   I'll find the one that does –

(*Finally noticing* **Meek**.) Hey, MeekMeek.

Meek   Gran'ma, Aunt Virgie been in the bathroom a long time.

Puddin   Thank you, baby. Go'n and take that trash out 'fore ya father gets home.

Meek *leaves.*

Clay   You got her watching Virgie?

Puddin   You tell me what's really goin' on with her and I wouldn't have to.

Clay   The situation is delicate, Ma –

Puddin   Boy, if you don't tell me what the hell is goin on.

Clay   Virgie was involved with this group, Wellspring . . .

Puddin   Wellspring?

Clay   They make their members do things . . .

Puddin   What kind of things?

Clay   The kinds of things that could have put her in a bad spot – put both of us in a bad spot, but I got her out, she was messed up, but I got her out. She was doing better, and then last week she disappeared. I'm afraid they got to her, but she won't say. Virgie's a mess. This shit with the Soviets is about to blow up in our face – I need your help. Can you please do this for me?

Puddin   Alright.

Clay   Thank you. (*Stopping short – the briefcase.*) Actually, is there somewhere I can put this? It has work stuff. Confidential stuff.

Puddin (*tossing the keys*)   The safe in Smooch's office. Better do it 'fore he gets back.

Clay   Combination?

Puddin   Meek's birthday.

Clay (Does he know it?)   . . .

Puddin (He better know it.)   . . .

Clay   Got it. Thanks, Ma.

Triple A

> **Meek** *brings the trash out to the bins behind the Roll-a-Rama. It's dark, the bags are heavy.* **Meek** *accidentally lets the door slam – it locks shut.*
>
> **Familiar Face** *appears with gloves and a duffle bag.*

Familiar Face   That looks heavy. Need a hand?

Meek   No.

> **Familiar Face** *steps forward.* **Meek** *steps back.*

Meek   You're not supposed to be back here.

Familiar Face   Says who?

Meek   My daddy. Nobody supposed to be hanging out back here.

Familiar Face   I'm not hanging out. I heard someone's having car trouble.

Meek   Who are you?

Familiar Face   I'm with Triple A and I'm guessing that car out front is the one I'm here to see. Do you know who it belongs to?

Meek   Uncle Clay and Aunt Virgie. She in a cult.

Familiar Face   Oh yeah? Did she tell you that?

Meek   Uncle Clay was going to call Triple A.

Familiar Face   Here I am.

Meek   But Gran'ma said don't none of them phones work.

Familiar Face   Well, they must've fixed one of them, because here I am.

Meek   . . .

Familiar Face   He told me you'd be here. He said I should ask you to help me find his wife. She needs help bringing their luggage down. He wants her ready to go as soon as the car is fixed. Can you help me find his wife? He said you'd be a good helper.

> **Familiar Face** *steps forward.*
>
> **Meek** *steps back, tries the door. Still locked.*
>
> **Familiar Face** *steps closer.*

Familiar Face   Are you going to be a good helper?

> **Smooch** *comes around back.*

Smooch   MeekMeek – Can I help you?

Familiar Face   I'm with Triple A. I'm looking for the owner of that car out front.

Smooch   Well, he ain't back here.

Familiar Face   No, he's not.

Smooch   He'll be back soon.

Familiar Face   Maybe I'll just wait for him inside.

Smooch   Nah, you ain't doin' that.

Familiar Face   Okay.

Smooch   Anything else?

Familiar Face   No. Nothing else.

> **Familiar Face** *leaves.*

Smooch   If you see that person again, I want you to let me know right away. Okay?

Meek   Okay.

Smooch   All power to who?

Meek   The people.

Smooch   That's right. You my people. You see how I stepped in for you? You always gotta look out for your family, Meek. Don't be like your whack ass uncle.

Meek   Okay.

Smooch   . . .

Meek   Daddy? You alright, Daddy?

Smooch   Yeah. Yeah, I'm alright. Come on inside.

> *They go inside. After a moment*
> **Familiar Face** *reemerges,*
> *jimmies the lock, and slips inside.*

Very Good Friend

> **Puddin** *flips through channels on the TV and cleans.*

Puddin   You took that trash out?

Meek   Yes, Gran'ma.

> **Barbara Walters** (*on TV*) This is *Twenty-Twenty*. . .
>
> Tonight an exclusive interview with a survivor of the Wellspring Group.
>
> **Puddin** *stops cleaning to watch.* **Meek** *finds her* **Speak + Spell**. **The Choir** *emerges from the dark around her.*
>
> **The Choir**
> AH AH AH
> AH AH AH AH AH AH
> AH AH AH
> AH AH AH AH AH AH

Meek   Hello? Are you there?

Speak + Spell   I am here, Meeksnaya.

Meek   I'll do it. I'll meet your friend.

Speak + Spell   Kharasho. At seven o'clock there will be a bus.

> *A bus appears.* **The Choir**, *now passengers, sing.*
>
> **The Choir**
> TOVARISHCH
> MEEKSNAYA,
> TOVARISHCH
> MEEKSNAYA RODINA

VIDIT TEBYA. RODINA
VIDIT TEBYA.

Speak + Spell   The bus will take you to Green Lakes State Park. At the park there will be a forest trail.

Meek *walks along the trail.*

Speak + Spell   You will meet a hiker on this trail. She will ask you . . .

Hiker   Vashi dokumenty?

Speak + Spell   You will answer . . .

Meek   Pasport.

Speak + Spell   The hiker will walk ahead of you.

The Choir
OOH OOH OOH OOH
OOH OOH OOH OOH

Speak + Spell   You will follow her to a cabin and knock twice.

Meek *knocks twice.*

Speak + Spell   Inside you will find my Very Good Friend . . .

Very Good Friend   You are late. Sit.

Meek   Why are we meeting all the way out here?

Very Good Friend   We need to speak without little mice listening in walls.

Znayesh', pochemu ty zdes'?

Speak + Spell   She will ask if you know why you are here.

Meek (*fluent*)   Mne skazali, chto ya mogu pomoch' Rodini, a Rodina mozhet pomoch' mne.

Very Good Friend   I am impressed by your Russian.

That will be useful now that you've decided to work with us.

Meek   I haven't decided anything.

I don't even know what you want me to do.

Speak + Spell   You will be cautious. It is good to be cautious, but my friend will show you this is simple thing.

Very Good Friend   Next week in Washington a summit is scheduled with your president and –

Meek   Mikhail Gorbachev. Uncle Clay says he might not come.

Very Good Friend   Correct. Your uncle has been central to development of U.S. nuclear strategy.

Clay *appears*.

Very Good Friend   The U.S. wants to limit weapons.

We want this too, but we do not trust the Americans.

General Secretary Gorbachev will not come to sign treaty unless we know the Americans will do as they say they will do.

Meek   What does that have to do with me?

Very Good Friend   You want peace. Peace is not a song you sing.

Peace is one friend helping other friend.

You are close to him, you can help us.

Meek   We're not close, he barely notices me.

Very Good Friend   Exactly. He will not notice.

Speak + Spell   Use this to your advantage, comrade.

Very Good Friend   U nego yest' portfel'.

Vnutri portfelya lezhat dokumenty, kotoryye nam nuzhny.

Speak + Spell   'He has a briefcase.

Inside are the documents we need to see.'

/ Top secret.

Very Good Friend   Top secret.

Speak + Spell   On a normal day he would take great care with such documents.

> **Clay** *holds his briefcase to his chest.*

> **Very Good Friend**   Today not normal day.

> **Virgie** *appears next to* **Clay**.

Speak + Spell   Today he is distracted by wife with strange relationship to water.

> **Very Good Friend**   Ona chlen opasnoy gruppy.

Speak + Spell   Be careful of her.

She is part of a dangerous group that seeks the same documents.

> **Very Good Friend**   Ty voz'myosh portfel' i zaberesh dokumenty.

Speak + Spell   You must get there first.

'Take the briefcase and bring us the documents.'

> **Meek**   My gran'ma said I shouldn't be doing dangerous stuff.

> I shouldn't even be here.

Speak + Spell   You will consider the danger.

And of course your grandmother is right.

But what is more dangerous than being alone in a world that uses the weak as fuel to spin on its axis?

> **Meek**   But how would I even do all this?

> **Very Good Friend**   You must wait for moment to slip away.

The briefcase is in secure location inside roller rink.

Do you know where that may be?

Meek   I think so, but –

Very Good Friend   Help a friend, Meeksnaya.

Meek   I have to go –

Very Good Friend (*a hardening*)   You will not help us, comrade?

Speak + Spell   You will leave my Very Good Friend.

> **Meek** *goes down the trail, back to the bus.*

Speak + Spell   You will arrive home.

> **Meek** *arrives at the Roll-a-Rama.*

Smooch (*off-stage*)   MeekMeek! Time to eat!

Speak + Spell   No one will have noticed you were gone.

And then you will decide . . .

> **The Choir**
> AH AH AH!

Been Away Too Long

> *The bathroom.* **Familiar Face**
> *surprises* **Virgie.**

Familiar Face   Hey there, Virgie. I drove a long way to get to you.

Virgie   How did you know I was here?

Familiar Face   I can always find you. You know that. I have a directive for you.

Your husband has documents in his possession that are of interest to the group.

Virgie   What kind of documents?

Familiar Face   Work documents.

Virgie   But that would be classified –

Familiar Face   They weren't in his office and they weren't at your home. Is it possible they're on his person?

Virgie   You searched our home? –

Familiar Face   Maybe in a briefcase? Did he bring his briefcase with him?

Virgie   Um, yes. He did.

Familiar Face   Good. Bring it to me.

Virgie   Is this about the White House summit?

Familiar Face   You've been away too long. You don't ask questions, you follow directives.

Virgie   I'm sorry. It's just – if it's something involving Clay's work – I – I don't want to hurt his position–

Familiar Face   And what about our position? When you left you stole something from every person in the group. You stole our progress, our potential. I brought you back into the fold, you begged for a chance to make amends, and then you disappeared again. Some members of the group are starting to question your loyalty.

Virgie   I'm – I'm loyal. I just don't want to hurt my husband.

Familiar Face   Have you told him anything?

Virgie   No.

Familiar Face   Good. I'm giving you one chance to get this right.

> *A knocking from outside the bathroom.*
>
> **Clay** (*off stage*)   Virgie? You in there?

Familiar Face   Get the briefcase. Page me when you have it.

> **Clay** (*off stage*)   Virgie? Is it okay to come in?
>
> **Familiar Face** *slips past* **Clay** *as he enters.*

Clay   Hey, everything okay?

Virgie   Yes. . . I'm – I'm feeling so much better now.

Clay (*unconvinced*)   Good. That's really good to hear. Who was that?

Virgie   I don't know.

> *A familiar melody creeps into* **Virgie**'s *ear.*

Clay
I thought I heard you talking.

The Choir (*as 'the group'*)
OOH OOH OOH. . .

Virgie   No.

Clay   Hon, if I ask you something, would you answer me honestly?

Virgie   I'm always honest with you.

Clay   When you disappeared that night, were you with the group?

Virgie   Uh. . . I –

Clay   In treatment they told us how these groups operate. They never just let people go. So if they've made contact, that's something I need to know.

> *As if she never left,* **Familiar Face** *haunts the bathroom, taking the reigns.*
>
> **Familiar Face**   I wasn't with the group.

Virgie   I wasn't with the group.

Clay   If you weren't with the group, who were you with that night?

> **Familiar Face**   I don't remember.

Virgie   I don't remember –

Clay   I thought you were feeling better.

Virgie   I am –

Clay   THEN TELL ME THE TRUTH.

I'm sorry. I just need you to trust me.

> **Familiar Face**   I wasn't with the group. They haven't made contact.

Virgie   I wasn't with the group. They haven't made contact.

Clay   Promise?

Virgie	**Familiar Face**
Promise.	Promise.

Clay   I want you to stay close to me while I figure this car stuff out.

Virgie   What about our things – your briefcase?

Clay   It's secure. I locked it in Smooch's office.

Adult Skate Night

Inside the Roll-a-Rama. **Meek** *finishes a dinner of fries and soda pop. The TV plays clips from Reagan's speech at Brandenburg Gate.*[4]

Reagan Audio   In the West today, we see a free world that has achieved a level of prosperity and well-being unprecedented in all human history.

Smooch *examines some damage to a wall.*

Looks like mold.

Reagan Audio   In the Communist world, we see failure.

Smooch *slaps a coat of paint over the damage.*

Reagan Audio   General Secretary Gorbachev, if you seek prosperity for the Soviet Union and Eastern Europe. Mr. Gorbachev, tear down this wall! Tear down this wall . . .

---

[4] 'Remarks on East-West Relations at the Brandenburg Gate in West Berlin June 12, 1987.' The Public Papers of President Ronald W. Reagan. Ronald Reagan Presidential Library. www.reaganlibrary.gov/archives/public-papers-president-ronald-reagan (accessed December 2022).

Pleased with the patchwork **Smooch** *puts his gear away. The lights dim and the beat . . . drops.*

The Choir*, now background vocalists, sings the hook. . .*

The Choir
AH! AH!
TEAR DOWN THIS WALL!
TEAR DOWN THIS WALL!
AH! AH!
TEAR DOWN THIS WALL!
TEAR DOWN THIS WALL!

The doors open and patrons stroll in. Young, old, and all Black. Five dollars to skate. Two dollars to rent. **Meek** *works the rentals,* **Smooch** *the turntables.*

Smooch (*on the mic*)   It's about that time . . . Adult Skate Night!

Smooch *takes the floor and skates. He narrates all text that isn't sung by* **The Choir**.

Smooch   A constellation of neon lights appears.

A thousand galaxies birthing another thousand galaxies

of orange, pink, and electric boogaloo blue.

The Choir
AH! AH!
TEAR DOWN THIS WALL!
TEAR DOWN THIS WALL!

Smooch   The smell of pizza pies and once frozen fries. The sound of wheels on wood.

The feel of custom skates made from fresh

Jordan's on silver plates.

The improbable combo of winter coats

and booty shorts.

> **Choir**
> AAAH!
> AAAH!
> AAAAAAH!

Smooch   Skaters take the floor.   Alone   together.

Skating 'round and 'round the invisible pinpoint in the center of the rink.

The best ones stick to the edges where only the fast and the
fly belong.

Gran'ma on her skates. Auntie on hers too. Get it!!!

Smooch emerges from the stars like a great Black COMET.

He skates!

He floats!

He flies!

They hit the middle to dance. Smooch leads the way.

His night,

his moves,

his groove. . .

Now you can chill in this groove if you
want to. Why the fuck not?

NASA, ESA, CSA, STScI; Joseph DePasquale (STScI), Anton M. Koekemoer (STScI), Alyssa Pagan (STScI)

Mister Black Republican

> **Clay** *and* **Virgie** *push through the crowd. They are wildly out of place. Mistletoe in May.*
>
> **Smooch** *holds court in the rink.*

Smooch   Look who it is! Brotha Clay! –

What I tell you 'bout comin' up in here?

Clay   I'm using your phone. And I swear to god if you try and stop me –

Smooch   Whatchu gonna do?

Puddin   Okay, now. We got customers.

Clay (*to* **Virgie**)   Sit right here, I'll only be a minute.

Smooch   Why she gotta sit? It's Skate Night, baby! Meek, get 'em some skates.

Clay   Phone?

Puddin   By the canteen.

Smooch   That's a man on a mission. Got that official White House business! Mister Black Republican!

(*To the crowd.*)   Oh, y'all ain't know that? Oh yeah! This here is Ronald Reagan's right testicle!

Puddin   Oh lord, / Smooch.

Clay   I don't care if you got a problem with my politics –

Smooch   Ain't no problem. Diversity makes the world go 'round. Ain't that right, Virgie?

Clay   Back off, man –

Smooch   Yeah, Clay, this ain't like them parties you go to up at the White House.

(*Gesturing around.*) Lotta negroes.

Clay   I said back off!

Smooch   Whatchu really doin' in that white man's house anyway? Huh? I bet they got ya Black ass tucked away in the basement, polishin' the silver while the real men get to work –

Clay   You think I'm playing with you?

> **Meek** *brings skates for* **Clay** *and* **Virgie**. **Clay** *takes off his shoes and puts on some skates.*

Virgie   Clay? –

Smooch   Oh, he mad now! Look at him.

Virgie   Clay, / what are you doing?

Puddin   Clay, I think you betta calm down –

Smooch   You tryin' to come in here? –

Clay   Yeah, I'm coming in –

Virgie   / Do you think that's a good idea? –

Puddin   I don't think you should do that –

Smooch   You gonna take them knee socks off?

Puddin   Clay, go'n and use the phone and cut this mess out –

Clay   Talkin all that shit, I'm about to show your motherfuckin' ass.

Smooch   Whatchu say? Speak up, bruh!

> **Clay** *steps in. It's been a minute.*
> *He struggles to get his bearings.*

Smooch   Don't fall! –

Virgie   / Clay, please!

Puddin   Clay, you gon' hurt yourself! –

Clay   I'm not going to hurt myself! –

Smooch   You betta listen to ya mama –

Clay   I KNOW HOW TO FUCKING SKATE.

> *It's coming back to him. He shows off a bit. He's good, but not as good as* **Smooch***. They circle each other in the rink . . .*

Clay   I taught your little nappy headed ass.

Smooch   Nah. Don't do that. / Don't do that.

Clay   Don't do what? I taught you everything you know. I practically raised you –

Smooch   No, *Ma* raised me!

Clay   You're so fucking ungrateful!

Smooch   What I'm supposed to be grateful for??? You teachin' me how to skate? –

Clay   I taught you how to be a man!

Smooch   You don't know nothin' 'bout that. You got me to join the Panthers. You was talkin' family this, community that, the white man this – AND THEN THE FIRST CHANCE YOU GET . . . the first fuckin' crumb they throw yo' black ass . . . you gone. You don't know me. You don't know Ma. And I'm supposed to be grateful???

Clay   I made you a roadmap! / I taught you how to be successful. You didn't fuckin listen!

Smooch   A roadmap?! HAHAHA WHOOO. To the White House? Nigga, please . . . I don't need a fuckin' roadmap!

I need my brother! Where the fuck you been, man? Huh? Where the fuck you been?

Clay   . . .

Smooch   Get the fuck out my roller rink.

> **Clay** *doesn't move.*

Smooch   I said get the fuck out!

> **Clay** *still doesn't move.* **Smooch**
> *pushes* **Clay** *hard. They tussle.*
> *Locked onto each other, spinning*
> *like one unit.*

Virgie (*over the fighting*)   Clay! Please come out of there /
right now. Clay! Please stop this! Please!

Puddin (*over the fighting*)   Smooch! Stop this mess right now.
Both of you betta stop fightin! I said that's enough!

> *What happens next is a violence.*
> *It can be abstract, dance,*
> *whatever, but it's a violence.*
> **Smooch** *lands the last blow.*

Virgie   Oh my god, Clay!

Clay   You broke my fucking jaw!

Smooch   If you talkin' ya jaw ain't broke.

Virgie   Are you okay?

Clay (*so not*)   I'm fine.

Puddin   Meek! Get me some frozen peas!

> **Meek** *is long gone.*

Puddin   Meek!

Ambitious Professionals

> **Smooch**'s *back office. Complete darkness. Music from Adult Skate Night bleeds into the room.*
>
> *Keys wriggle in the lock.*
>
> **Click**
>
> *A pen light flicks on. The light scans the space before landing on the safe. They open the safe and pull out* **Clay**'s *briefcase and shuffle through papers.*
>
> *The doorknob jiggles. The pen light flicks off. An unpracticed hand pries at the lock, makes a clumsy job of it. The door opens and the person slides in. Groping around the dark until they find the light switch.*
>
> **Virgie** *startles* **Meek** *in the light.*

Virgie   . . .

Meek   . . .

Virgie   What are you doing in here?

Meek   What are you doing in here?

Virgie   . . .

Meek   . . .

Virgie   That's your uncle's briefcase. I'll take that, thank you.

Meek   It doesn't belong to you.

Virgie   We're married. If it belongs to him, it belongs to me. Give it to me.

Meek   Why do you want it?

Virgie   Your uncle asked for it.

Meek   Ty lzhyósh!

Virgie   What?

Meek   You're a liar!

Virgie   . . . Did your Soviet friend tell you to take that briefcase, Meek?

Meek   My Soviet friend told me to watch out for you. She told me *you'd* be looking for the briefcase.

Virgie   I hope that's not true, Meek. Because that would mean, you're helping the enemy. And your uncle and I would have to tell the president. And then you'd be in big big trouble. You're lucky I found you, this is too much to handle on your own.

Meek   I'm not on my own, I have many friends! The Soviet Union has many friends! We're saving the world!

Virgie   There is no version of saving the world that includes helping the Soviet Union.

Give me the briefcase –

Meek   Get away from me! –

Virgie   Give it to me or I'll have to give you a spanking!

Meek   Touch me and I'll scream!

Virgie   No one can hear you down here.

Meek   No one can hear you either.

> **Virgie** *pries the briefcase from* **Meek***, but not without getting bitten first.*

Virgie   DAMMIT.

> **Meek** *runs out.*

> **Virgie** *picks up the phone and dials a pager number. She finds the number to the Roll-a-Rama on* **Smooch**'s *desk and punches it in. She hangs up and waits.*
>
> *After a moment the phone rings . . .*

Virgie   I have it.

. . . basement level, there's an office –

> **Puddin** *appears in the office doorway.*

Puddin   Can I help you find something?

Virgie   No, no. I was just – I just – I needed the phone.

Puddin (*off the damaged lock*)   I could've given you the key.

Virgie   It was an emergency.

Puddin   What's the emergency?

Virgie   The fighting. I was scared. I was going to – I don't know what I was going to do.

Puddin   That Clay's briefcase.

Virgie   It is.

Puddin   How'd you open the safe?

Virgie   I didn't. Meek must've opened it –

Puddin   I know my grandbaby ain't do nothing like that –

Virgie   I don't get the sense that you're keeping a close eye on her. It's troubling.

Puddin   You wanna talk about troublin? We can talk about troublin. Tell me, you ever watch *Twenty-Twenty*?

Virgie   No.

Puddin   Oh, that's my show! Puddin don't miss *Twenty-Twenty*. You would've liked this week's episode.

> **Barbara Walters**   Tonight we bring you a first-hand account of a powerful and secretive organization operating in our nation's capital.

Puddin   One of them big time cults –

Virgie   Why would I have liked that?

Puddin   Oh, I forgot you ain't in a cult, you in a 'group'.

Well, Barbara had on this ghostly lookin' girl.

> **Young Woman** *appears in an interview chair.*
>
> **Young Woman**   I was a member of Wellspring for about three years.
>
> It was a group for ambitious professionals.

Puddin   Now as the interview went on this girl gets an itch in her throat and starts suckin' down water.

Who that sound like?

> **Young Woman**   It's part of my recovery.
>
> Water regulation is how Wellspring controlled us.

Virgie   That sounds horrible. I feel sorry for her.

Puddin   I do too. 'Cause they had her involved in some serious stuff.

See now, the founder of Wellspring is also the CEO of the biggest arms manufacturer in the country.

> **Young Woman**   They make ballistic missiles for the U.S.

Virgie   That can't be right – that doesn't make any sense –

Puddin   That's what I said. Why would an arms dealer start a group for spooky women? But then you look at who they was recruiting . . .

> **Young Woman**   Most of the women they recruited worked on the hill, or had connections there.
>
> **Puddin** *goes into full Jessica Fletcher mode.*

Puddin   Mutually Assured Destruction is a gold mine. But now Reagan wants arms control, which can get in the way of that gold mine. So they used ambitious professionals, well connected women to do all the dirty work that would keep them government contracts flowin' in. And who's more well-connected than the wife of the Deputy National Security Advisor!

Virgie   I don't like what you're insinuating –

Puddin   That's why they recruited you, Virgie, isn't it? You're married to Clay –

Virgie   You don't know what you're talking about –

Puddin   They knew Clay was working on that treaty, so they sent you in here, / didn't they, Virgie?

Virgie   No. No. That's not what this is! –

Puddin   See you ain't know ya mama-in-law was sharp as a jack knife! Puddin sees *everything*! I know the real reason you in here, runnin' up my water bill witcha itchy throat! Puttin' your sticky fingers on government secrets! OH YOU IN A CULT ALRIGHT! (*Snatching the briefcase.*) Now you gon' tell Clay whatchu up to or am I?

Virgie   Puddin, you have to believe me. I had no idea. / I would never jeopardize Clay's work –

Puddin (*dialing the phone*)   Mmm hmm . . . oh yeah sure, Virgie –

Virgie   What are you doing?

Puddin   I'm calling the police –

Virgie (*slamming the phone*)   You can't do that. If I don't do what they say, they will hurt you. They will hurt me. They will hurt Clay – that can't happen –

A knock on the door.

Familiar Face   Virgie? Open the door.

Puddin   That's your little cult friend. She coming for this, ain't she?

Virgie   Be quiet.

Familiar Face *tries the door.*

Familiar Face   I can hear you talking. Who's in there with you?

Virgie	**Puddin**
. . .	. . .

Familiar Face   Open the door now!

Puddin   We ain't openin' shit!

Familiar Face *jimmies the lock
and steps inside wearing gloves
and carrying a duffel bag.*

Puddin   I knew it! Did I call it or did I call it?

Familiar Face   Who is this?

Virgie   My mother-in-law.

Puddin   No, I'm the one who figured this whole thing out. Y'all need to step it up 'cause I put that together real quick –

Virgie   Please be quiet, Puddin –

Familiar Face   What did you tell her?

Virgie   Nothing –

Puddin   Everything!

I know you in a cult.

I know you messin' with my son's paycheck.

I know you 'bout to be arrested for breakin' and enterin' and snatchin' up nuclear secrets –

> **Familiar Face** *pulls out a gun.*

Familiar Face   The briefcase. Open it.

> **Virgie** *opens the briefcase. It's empty.*

Familiar Face   Where the fuck are the documents?

Virgie   I – don't – I don't know – they should be here –

Puddin   That's what you get sneakin' around –

Familiar Face   Stop talking. Both of you sit.

Puddin   I can't be sittin' on the floor, my knees ain't good –

Familiar Face   Sit.

> **Puddin** *and* **Virgie** *sit.*
> **Familiar Face** *makes a call.*

Familiar Face (*on the phone*)   They're not here . . . and we have another problem . . . I'm cleaning it up now.

Puddin   'Cleanin' it up'? What she 'bout to do?

Familiar Face   Quiet. Over there. . .

Virgie   If I can just talk to him, / I can figure out where they are.

Familiar Face   Hands behind your back.

> **Familiar Face** *ties* **Virgie** *and*
> **Puddin** *together, back-to-back at*
> *the wrists,*

Puddin   Whatchu tryin' to clean up? –

Familiar Face   I said shut up!

Puddin (*to* **Familiar Face**)   Who you talkin' to like that –

Virgie   Puddin, please. / I think you should listen.

Familiar Face   What are you not understanding?

Puddin   Virgie, you betta get ya friend –

Familiar Face   I SAID SHUT YOUR GODDAMN
MOUTH!

You compromised the safety of the unit and now you have to
make it right.

> **Familiar Face** *pulls a sleek black*
> *box from her duffel bag. She*
> *handles it with great care.*

Puddin   What is that?   **Virgie**   Please don't do this.

Familiar Face   You have all you need to see this through to
the end. Say it.

Virgie   I have all I need to   **Puddin** (*to* **Familiar Face**)
see this through to the end.   What do you mean see it
                                  through to the end? Hello?
                                  I know you hear me!

> **Familiar Face** *sets the timer on*
> *the box and leaves.*

Virgie   / I have all I need to see this through to the end.

I have all I need to see this through to the end.

I have all I need to see this through to the end.

I have all I need to see this through to the end.

Puddin (*over* **Virgie**)   HELP!!! HELP ME! SMOOCH! CLAY! SOMEBODY!!! HELP!!!

You Ain't Got To Go

Out back, behind the Roll-a-Rama. **Clay** *sits nursing his jaw with a pack of frozen peas.*

Smooch *brings out a couple of beers.*

Clay   Thanks.

Smooch   . . .

Clay   . . .

They drink in silence.

Clay   I don't even know what time it is.

Smooch   Late.

Clay   Where's Virgie?

Smooch   Probably up in the apartment with Ma.

Clay   I'd better go wake her. Find a hotel or something –

Smooch   You ain't got to go.

Take my room, I'll sleep on the couch.

Clay   I appreciate that.

Smooch   . . .

Clay   . . .

Smooch   You know it took me three years to buy this place. I was working two jobs, six days a week, the whole time savin' and savin'. The place didn't hardly cost nothin' and that shit still took three years.

Clay   I wish you would've talked to me first. I would've told you it was a bad investment.

Smooch   I didn't buy this shit for no investment. I bought it 'cause I knew I could make it like it used to be when we was kids.

Clay   So nostalgia? –

Smooch   Nah, nigga. This place was everything. We used to come here for free breakfast in the mornings, Panther meetings at night, skatin' with shorties on the weekend. This place was the spot. We need something like that again. That's why I'm doin' it. 'Black folks need to do for themselves.' Psh. We need to do for our community. I'm doin' this for us. Whatchu doin'?

Clay   A lot. That shit we did in our twenties. That wasn't a game to me. It's just . . . I don't know. I got to law school and realized that 'Black Power', all that shit. That's a slogan. That's a poster. It's not real, Smooch. What I'm doing now. . . that's real power. That's the shit you can't touch unless you get real close – and I'm right fucking there. That's what I'm doing.

Smooch   . . .

Clay   . . .

Smooch   It's weird, man . . . feelin' like I don't even know my own brother.

Clay   I'm the same person –

Smooch   You know that's not true.

Clay   I'm grabbing a rental car in the morning.

If you don't mind dropping us off?

Smooch   When you comin' back?

Clay   I don't know. Work is . . .

And Virgie needs me right now –

Smooch   What about your family?

Clay   Virgie is my family.

Smooch   . . .

Clay   . . .

Smooch   . . .

Clay   We'll be out of your hair in the morning.

All You Need

> **Smooch***'s office.* **Puddin** *and* **Virgie** *are still tied together. The device is ticking away, but the voices of 'the group' drill into* **Virgie***'s ear, taunting her.*
>
> **The Choir** (*as group members*)
> ALL YOU NEED
> YOU HAVE ALL YOU. . .
>
> **Puddin** *tries to wriggle out of the ropes. No luck.*

Puddin (*over singing*)	Virgie (*over singing*)	Singers One and Two	Singer Three
. . .	you will see this through to the end	NEED	YOU HAVE ALL YOU NEED
Virgie? Excuse me, Virgie?	you are lucky	YOU HAVE	YOU HAVE ALL YOU NEED
Who are you talking to?	you will deliver	YOU	WHAT YOU NEED YOU
. . .	you have all you need	HAVE	HAVE WITHIN IN
Do you? Do you have *all* you need?	you have all you need	ALL	YOU HAVE
'Cause personally I need to get the	you have all you need	YOU	ALL YOU NEED YOU HAVE
hell out of this room!	you have all you need	NEED	YOU HAVE ALL YOU NEED
Virgie!! Lord Jesus this child	You are lucky.	YOU HAVE	YOU HAVE ALL YOU NEED
done lost her damn mind!	This will be quick.	YOU	WHAT YOU NEED YOU
We gotta get out of here! SNAP OUT OF IT!!!	You have all you need –	HAVE –	HAVE WITHIN IN –

Silence.

Puddin   Virgie, I need you to come on back to Earth.

Virgie   I . . . I can't . . .

Puddin   I shoulda let you drink that water. I see that now.

Virgie   I – I can't hear my own thoughts –

Puddin   I bet. I know that wasn't you talkin. Now we gotta get outta here before that thing goes off–

Virgie   We're gonna die in here! / We're gonna die!

Puddin   No no, Virgie! We ain't doin' that –

Virgie   We are! And it's my fault–

Puddin   It's not your fault – it's not all your fault. The way them folks used you wasn't right.

Virgie   They said not drinking would prove our strength. I wanted to be the strongest. The other girls got so desperate, sneaking water from the bathroom sinks – but I never broke. They said I could do big things, / that I had potential.

Puddin   Hey, Virgie, I'm sorry, but we gotta go. We gotta find Smooch and Clay –

Virgie   Oh god, when Clay finds out –

Puddin   Clay's not gonna find out, 'cause ain't neither one of us gonna tell him. You got my word on that. NOW GET UP! ONE-TWO-THREE!

*They make it to their feet without
a second to lose . . .*

Puddin   We gotta cut these ties. Meek's got an emergency kit there on the desk.

Virgie   There's a paper bag –

Puddin   That's an emergency kit. See if it's got something inside to cut these ties with?

Virgie   There's lots of snacks –

Puddin   Something sharp! –

Virgie   There's a box cutter!

Puddin   Grab it!

> *They do what they need to do*
> *physically to get **Virgie**'s hand*
> *down in the bag.*

Virgie   I got it! I got it! –

Puddin   Hurry up now, Virgie!

Virgie   Please don't be short with me! –

Puddin   I'm sorry Virgie! We only 'bout to be blown to bits by a goddamn bomb!

> *They free themselves.*

Virgin   Oh my god!   **Puddin**   Thank you, Jesus!

> **Virgie** *makes for the door, but*
> **Puddin** *eyes the device.*

Virgie   Puddin, come on! We gotta get everyone out!

Puddin   No. There's not enough time.

. . . I'm gonna take it out.

Virgie   Don't touch it!

Puddin   This is gonna take down the whole building –

Virgie   We have to go! –

Puddin   We leave then what? No. I gotta take it out.

Virgie   No. I'll do it. It's here because of me. I'll take it out.

Puddin   You sure?

Virgie   Yes. I'll take it out –

Puddin   Well, I ain't gonna argue witcha.

Virgie *takes a massive swig of water.*

Virgie   Give it to me.

Puddin *hands over the device carefully.*

Puddin   Not too fast. Real easy with it.

Virgie *moves slowly towards the door.*

Puddin   Little bit faster.

Virgie *picks up the pace and leaves.*

Special Warmth

South Salina Street.

Virgie *walks carefully into the dark with the device. Her hands shake, but she keeps moving forward, one foot, then the next.*

The Choir *underscores her walk.*

The Choir
SPECIAL WARMTH,
SPECIAL BEAUTY
OOH OOH OOH
OOH OOH OOH OOH

Singer One	Singer Two	Singer Three
DING DONG DING DONG DING	HAPPY HAPPY HAPPY TIDINGS	SPECIAL BEAUTY
DING DING DING DING	HAPPY HAPPY HAPPY TIDINGS	SPECIAL WARMTH
LA LA LA LA LA LA	LA LA LA LA LA LA	LA LA LA LA LA LA
LA LA LA	LA LA LA	LA LA LA
LA LA LA LA	LA LA LA LA	LA LA LA LA
DING DONG DING DONG DING	HAPPY HAPPY HAPPY TIDINGS	SPECIAL BEAUTY
DING DING DING DING	HAPPY HAPPY HAPPY TIDINGS	SPECIAL WARMTH
LA LA LA LA LA LA	LA LA LA LA LA LA	LA LA LA LA LA LA
LA LA LA	LA LA LA	LA LA LA
LA LA LA LA	LA LA LA LA	LA LA LA LA

Virgie *sets the device down and runs like hell.*

The Choir
ALL YOU NEED

YOU HAVE ALL YOU –

An explosion.

The concrete on South Salina Street jolts up. Buildings convulse. A different kind of light creeps across the sky as flames eat the night.

Virgie *falls injured.*

Fill Up Midnight

> **Meek** *sits alone with the* **Speak + Spell***.*

Speak + Spell   Comrade, we have reports of an explosion. Are you alright?

Meek   Yeah.

Speak + Spell   Were you able to save the documents?

Meek   . . . My tooth hurts.

Speak + Spell   . . . Meeksnaya, do you have the documents?

Meek   I have a cavity. I'm not going to tell Daddy though. He told me 'bout 'eatin' all that candy'. When I can't sleep, I like to eat the Fireballs Mr. Davis gives me for shoveling his walkway. It helps me fall asleep. When it happened, I had one sitting in the back of my mouth against my teeth. I had mixed it with spit and made a swimming pool for my gums. It burned like chlorine. I gulped it down and imagined myself at the bottom of the pool, my bones sharp and razor thin. No chin or cheeks, just eyes and ears and tips of fingers, prying open secret places. Disappearing inside.

> **The Choir** *enters underscoring the scene with singing.*

Meek   The explosion was so loud. Loud like an atomic bomb. Everything was shaking. I was screaming, I was so scared – but I couldn't run, I couldn't breathe, I didn't know where my daddy was, where my gran'ma was. I thought I was too late. Then I saw through the window it wasn't a nuke, it was Mr. Davis' shop. I watched it flower out and fill up midnight. I watched it bathing in the blaze like a little bird, preening, then folding, buckling at the beams, drifting under.

> *Atomic Fireball candies descend from the sky.*

Meek	Singers One and Two	Singer Three
I watched the little rocks cascade down.	OOH OOH OOH OOH	BOM BOM BOM BOM BOM BOM BOM BOM
Like rain, but not. Like hail, but not. Burning, blazing red, sticky sweet and sharp like lake effect snowballs.	OOH	OOH OOH OOH
Jawbreakers, Atomic Fireballs, Molotov comets, cinnamon soaked	OOH OOH OOH OOH	BOM BOM BOM BOM BOM BOM BOM BOM
radioactive rubble bursting from the Candy Emporium.	OOH	OOH OOH OOH
Flaming, then falling, then staining the snow	OOH OOH	BOM BOM BOM BOM OOH OOH OOH
on South Salina Street.	AH AH	AH AH

The ground is littered with Fireballs.

Meek   Where were you?

Speak + Spell   I do not understand.

Meek   Peace is not a song you sing. You said we were friends, we were gonna help each other. Daddy has to close the Roll-a-Rama until everything is fixed, but how he gonna fix it with no money? How he gonna make money if it's closed? He said he's gonna help Mr. Davis rebuild – but how? There's nothing left to rebuild. Where were you?

Speak + Spell   I am here now, Meeksnaya and I am your friend. Do you have the documents?

Meek   Yes, I have the stupid documents.

Speak + Spell   You have done important thing. We will send someone to retrieve the documents and make arrangements for your family's departure.

Meek   I don't want to move to Russia anymore. I just want some money. For my dad. He needs money.

Speak + Spell   As you wish.

A Star Of Peace

The Roll-a-Rama's been through it. Shaken up, singed around the edges. The family holds the weight of this.

Meek *and* **Smooch** *sweep, while the Seedlings of Peace public access concert is on in the background.*

Choir Leader (*on the TV*)   We are the Syracuse, N.Y. chapter of the Seedlings of Peace. I'm so honored to lead this beautiful choir of children as they share their message of peace with the world . . . for exactly twenty-eight minutes.

Soloist One
LET'S BUILD ONE
AMERICA
ONE GLOBAL UNITED
STATES.

Soloist One + Two
OUR COUNTRY 'TIS OF
THEE
WE WILL GIVE YOU
LIBERTY

All
AND MARKETS THAT ARE
FREE!

Soloist Two
ONE GLOBAL AMERICA

Soloist One
WE ARE ONE AMERICA

<table>
<tr><td></td><td>Soloist One + Two
WE ARE ONE AMERICA</td></tr>
<tr><td>Soloist One + Two
WE ARE ONE AMERICA
WE ARE ONE AMERICA</td><td>Soloist Three
NO MORE WELFARE
NO MORE WELFARE</td></tr>
</table>

Smooch   How come you ain't wanna go to ya concert?

Meek   'Cause.

Smooch   Just 'cause?

Meek *shrugs.*

Smooch   Good. I never liked that choir. Got you singing them fucked up songs. Help me with these lights.

They untangle lights. **Puddin** *comes in with a box of Christmas decorations.*

Puddin   Alright, here go the decorations. Smooch, I can't find that tree.

Smooch   It's in the storage closet.

Puddin   I need a minute 'fore I go back up them stairs.

Smooch (*heading off*)   I got it, Ma.

Puddin *grabs the remote, flips to the news.*

Television   The White House announced today that it will not be renewing its contract with one of the nation's biggest arms manufacturers, citing treaty negotiations.

Puddin (*off the TV*)   Mmm hmm. That's what you get.

Meek   Gran'ma, what happened in Dad's office with Aunt Virgie?

Puddin   That's funny, I was wonderin' what happened in that office before I got there. Couldn't figure out how she got in ya daddy's safe.

Meek   . . . I guess there's some things we just won't know 'bout that night.

Puddin   I guess so.

> **Smooch** *returns with the tree.*

Puddin   Whatever happened, Virgie gon' be in that hospital a good long time.

Smooch   She lucky she alive. What the hell was she doin' outside anyway? You ain't see nothing that night?

Puddin   Meek and I fell asleep. We ain't see a thing. Ain't that right, Meek?

Meek   We ain't see nothin.

Smooch   I'm tellin' you, these pigs tryin to take us out.

Ma, come here for a sec.

> **Smooch** *pulls* **Puddin** *aside*
> *and takes out a thick envelope.*
> **Meek** *overhears.*

Smooch   You know anything about this?

Puddin   No.

Smooch   You ain't ask Clay for money?

Puddin   No. How much is it?

Smooch   Not enough. Cheap ass.

Meek   It's something, ain't it?

Smooch   What I tell you 'bout listenin' to grown folks talk –

Puddin   Nothin' wrong with takin' a peace offerin', get them windows fixed.

Smooch   If he wanted to make peace he would've stayed. Nah, I'm sending it back –

Meek   Why? It's not a peace offering. It's money. Uncle Clay ain't thinkin' 'bout us. Aunt Virgie ain't thinking 'bout us. The president ain't thinking 'bout us. Ain't nobody thinkin' 'bout us, but us. I'm tired of singing songs and building shelters, trying to be safe from everything – anything. Ain't no safe from. But this is something we can grab hold of, Daddy. We need it. It's here. Keep it.

Puddin   You heard that child. Keep it. That's enough of that. We gonna liven this place up. Let's watch 'em light that tree.

Puddin *flips through channels and lands on the National Tree Lighting Ceremony. They decorate the tree. President Reagan and an American Child materialize inside the Roll-a-Rama.*

The Choir
OOH OOH OOH OOH OOH

Reagan Audio   The lighting of the National Christmas Tree with its star of peace atop, could not come at a more symbolic moment.[5]

The Choir
OOH, A STAR OF PEACE ATOP A TREE.

[5] 'Remarks on Lighting the National Christmas Tree, December 7, 1987.' The Public Papers of President Ronald W. Reagan. Ronald Reagan Presidential Library. www.reaganlibrary.gov/archives/public-papers-president-ronald-reagan (accessed December 2022).

Reagan Audio   Two hours ago, General Secretary Gorbachev's plane touched down on American soil.

The Choir
GORBACHEV IS HERE!

Reagan Audio   He and I will meet in hopes of promoting peace for our peoples and all the people of the Earth.

Meek (*to TV* **Reagan**)   You're welcome.

The Choir
PEACE FOR ALL THE
PEOPLE OF THE EARTH

Puddin   MeekMeek, you seen the star?

Reagan Audio   I'd like him to see what we're celebrating. Peace on Earth. Good will toward men.

They look for the star, but the **American Child** *has it. The* **Choir** *hoists her high and she places it on the tree.*

Reagan Audio   I can't think of a better spirit in which to begin the meetings of the next several days.

The Choir (*under* **Reagan**)
OOH OOH OOH

Reagan Audio   As a small reminder of that spirit, the star of peace atop the national Christmas tree will be lit day and night during the time our Soviet guests are here.

Smooch *plugs the tree in, but the air is still heavy.*

Puddin   Okay, we ain't gon' be sulking through Christmas. Somebody gotta get in the spirit. Who gon' tell the story of Christmas this year?

The Choir
HAPPY HAPPY HAPPY
TIDINGS,
HAPPY HAPPY HAPPY
TIDINGS

Smooch   I'll tell it.

Meek   No, I'll tell it.

Smooch   Go 'head.   **Puddin**   Okay, baby.

Meek   There once was a child. A small child . . .

The Choir
MERRY MERRY MERRY,
MERRY MERRY MERRY

AAAAHHHH!
GORBACHEV!

The **Speak + Spell** *wakes, plays its three toned melody.*

End of Play.